Louisiana. Travel Guide (English)

World Guides Collection

Hank O'Connor

Table of Contents

1. General Information

Welcome to the Louisiana Travel Guide! Whether you're a first-time visitor or a seasoned traveler, Louisiana has something for everyone. From the vibrant city of New Orleans to the scenic bayous and historic plantations, this state is full of unique experiences and cultural attractions that are sure to leave a lasting impression.

In this guide, we'll take you through everything you need to know to plan an unforgettable trip to Louisiana. We've organized this guide into sections that cover each of the major elements of your trip, from getting around the state to exploring the top attractions and enjoying the local cuisine. Whether you're looking for recommendations on the best places to eat, drink, and dance the night away, or you're interested in the history and culture of this fascinating region, we've got you covered.

In this first chapter, we'll cover everything from the history of Louisiana to getting around the state. We'll also give you some tips on how to make the most of your budget and introduce you to the unique language and culture of Louisiana.

1.1. Brief History of Louisiana

Louisiana has a rich and varied history that spans thousands of years. The region was originally inhabited by several Native American tribes, including the Atakapa, Chitimacha, and Houma. In the 16th century, the region was explored by Spanish and French explorers, and by the 18th century, it had become a French colony.

One of the defining moments in Louisiana's history was the Louisiana Purchase, which took place in 1803. This was a landmark event in American history, as it doubled the size of the United States and gave the country control of the Mississippi River and the port of New Orleans.

Throughout the 19th and 20th centuries, Louisiana played a key role in the development of the United States. It was a major center for agriculture, particularly sugar cane, and was home to a large and diverse population of African Americans, who played a vital role in the development of jazz music.

1.2. Required Documentation

Before you start planning your trip to Louisiana, it's important to make sure you have all the necessary documentation. If you're a U.S. citizen, you won't need a visa to travel to Louisiana, but you will need a valid form of identification, such as a driver's license or passport.

If you're traveling from outside the United States, you may need a visa to enter the country. Check with your local U.S. embassy or consulate to find out what type of visa you need and how to apply.

It's also a good idea to check with your airline or travel agent to see if there are any additional requirements or restrictions for travel to Louisiana. Some airlines may require specific documentation or proof of vaccination before allowing you to board your flight.

In addition to your identification and travel documents, you may also want to bring a copy of your travel itinerary and any hotel reservations you've made. This can be helpful if you need to show proof of your travel plans to immigration or customs officials.

1.3. Getting There

Planning your trip to Louisiana can be an exciting experience, but it's important to make sure you have all the necessary information to get there safely and easily. Louisiana has several major airports, including Louis Armstrong New Orleans International Airport, which serves the city of New Orleans, and Baton Rouge Metropolitan Airport, which serves the capital city of Baton Rouge.

If you're driving to Louisiana, you'll find that the state has an extensive network of highways and interstates that make it easy to get around. The major interstate highways that run through Louisiana are I-10, I-12, I-20, and I-49. These highways connect Louisiana to major cities across the United States, including Houston, Dallas, Atlanta, and Miami.

If you're traveling by bus, Greyhound and Megabus both offer service to major cities in Louisiana. Amtrak also operates several train routes that pass through Louisiana, including the Crescent, which runs from New Orleans to New York City.

1.4. Getting Around

Getting around Louisiana can be an adventure in itself. From the bustling streets of New Orleans to the quiet bayous of the countryside, there are plenty of transportation options available to help you explore this fascinating state.

One of the most popular ways to get around Louisiana is by car. The state has an extensive network of highways and interstates that make it easy to get from one city to another. If you're renting a car, make sure to check the rental agreement carefully to understand any restrictions or fees that may apply.

If you prefer to travel by public transportation, Louisiana has several options available. The New Orleans Regional Transit Authority operates a network of buses and streetcars throughout the city, while the Capital Area Transit System serves the Baton Rouge metropolitan area. Greyhound and Megabus both offer bus service to major cities in Louisiana, and Amtrak operates several train routes that pass through the state.

Another popular way to explore Louisiana is by bike. The state has several dedicated bike trails, including the Tammany Trace, which runs from Covington to Slidell, and the Lafitte Greenway, which connects the French Quarter to Mid-City in New Orleans.

If you're looking for a more unique way to get around, consider taking a swamp tour. These tours take you through the bayous and wetlands of Louisiana, giving you a chance to see the state's natural beauty up close.

You can choose from guided tours on airboats, kayaks, or canoes, depending on your preferences.

1.5. Currency, Exchange and Budget

Before embarking on your trip to Louisiana, it's important to have a clear understanding of the currency, exchange rates, and budgeting expectations. The official currency of the United States is the U.S. Dollar (USD), and it is widely accepted throughout the state.

Most major credit cards, such as Visa, Mastercard, and American Express, are also widely accepted at hotels, restaurants, and tourist attractions. However, it's always a good idea to carry some cash with you, especially if you plan on visiting smaller shops or markets.

When it comes to budgeting for your trip, the cost of living in Louisiana can vary depending on the city and the type of accommodation you choose. New Orleans, for example, tends to be more expensive than other cities in the state, especially during peak tourist season.

In general, you can expect to pay around $100-150 per night for a mid-range hotel room in Louisiana, although prices can vary depending on the time of year and the location. If you're on a budget, consider staying in a hostel or Airbnb, which can be more affordable options.

When it comes to dining out, Louisiana is known for its delicious food and culinary scene. From Cajun and Creole dishes to fresh seafood and classic Southern fare, there's something for everyone to enjoy. Prices at restaurants can vary widely, but you can expect to pay around $15-25 for a mid-range meal, and more for fine dining experiences.

1.6. Language and Culture

Louisiana is home to a diverse population of people, including those of African American, Native American, and European descent. The state's culture is a blend of these diverse influences, resulting in a rich and vibrant tapestry of music, food, and traditions.

One of the most distinctive features of Louisiana's culture is its language. Louisiana is the only state in the United States where French is still widely spoken, particularly in the southern part of the state. Many Louisianans also speak a unique dialect of English that is influenced by French, Spanish, and African languages.

When you visit Louisiana, you'll have the opportunity to experience this unique blend of languages and cultures firsthand. From the music of New Orleans jazz to the spicy flavors of Cajun and Creole cuisine, there's something for everyone to enjoy.

Another important aspect of Louisiana's culture is its history. The state has a rich and varied past, with influences from Native American tribes, Spanish and French explorers, and African Americans who were brought to the state as slaves. As you travel through Louisiana, you'll see evidence of this history in the state's architecture, museums, and historic sites.

1.7. Louisiana in Popular Culture

Louisiana has long been a popular destination for filmmakers and television producers, thanks to its unique culture, architecture, and natural beauty. The state has been featured in countless films and TV shows over the years, from classic Hollywood movies like "Gone with the Wind" and "Streetcar Named Desire" to more recent productions like "True Blood" and "American Horror Story."

One of the most iconic images of Louisiana in popular culture is the Mardi Gras celebration, which takes place every year in New Orleans. This colorful event is known for its elaborate costumes, parades, and parties, and has been featured in numerous films and TV shows over the years.

Another popular aspect of Louisiana's culture is its music scene. The state is home to a vibrant and diverse music scene, with influences from jazz, blues, zydeco, and other genres. Famous musicians from Louisiana include Louis Armstrong, Fats Domino, and Harry Connick Jr.

Louisiana's food and drink culture is also well-known around the world. From classic Cajun and Creole dishes like gumbo and jambalaya to fresh seafood and spicy hot sauce, Louisiana's cuisine is a unique blend of flavors and influences. Visitors to the state can explore this delicious food culture by visiting local restaurants, cafes, and markets.

Finally, Louisiana is also known for its natural beauty and outdoor activities. From the bayous and swamps of the southern part of the state to the rolling hills and forests of the north, there's plenty to explore in Louisiana's great outdoors. Visitors can go fishing, hunting, birdwatching, or take a swamp tour to get up close and personal with the state's unique flora and fauna.

2. Major Cities

In this section, we'll take you on a tour of some of the state's most exciting cities, from the iconic streets of New Orleans to the charming downtown areas of Baton Rouge, Shreveport, Lafayette, and Lake Charles.

2.1. New Orleans

Welcome to New Orleans, one of the most iconic cities in the United States. Known for its exciting music scene, delicious cuisine, and colorful Mardi Gras celebrations, New Orleans is a city that's full of life and energy.

One of the most popular attractions in New Orleans is the French Quarter, a historic neighborhood that's home to some of the city's most famous landmarks, including

Jackson Square, St. Louis Cathedral, and the historic French Market. Visitors to the French Quarter can stroll down the colorful streets, listen to live music, and sample delicious food at some of the city's best restaurants and cafes.

Another must-visit attraction in New Orleans is Bourbon Street, a lively thoroughfare that's famous for its bars, nightclubs, and live music venues. Bourbon Street is a great place to experience the city's legendary nightlife and get a taste of the local culture.

If you're interested in learning about the history of New Orleans, be sure to visit the National WWII Museum, which is located in the city's Warehouse District. This museum is one of the most popular attractions in New Orleans and is dedicated to telling the story of World War II through interactive exhibits and immersive experiences.

For a taste of Louisiana's beautiful natural scenery, consider taking a swamp tour. These tours take you through the bayous and wetlands of the southern part of the state, giving you a chance to see alligators, birds, and other local wildlife up close.

2.2. Baton Rouge

Baton Rouge is the capital city of Louisiana, and is full of unique attractions and experiences that are sure to delight visitors of all ages.

One of the most iconic landmarks in Baton Rouge is the Louisiana State Capitol, which is located downtown and offers stunning views of the city and the Mississippi River. Visitors can take a guided tour of the capitol building, explore the beautiful grounds, and learn about the history of Louisiana's government.

If you're interested in the arts, be sure to visit the Shaw Center for the Arts, which is located in downtown Baton Rouge and features a range of galleries and performance spaces showcasing local and national talent. The center also offers classes and workshops in the visual and performing arts.

Another popular attraction in Baton Rouge is the USS Kidd, a World War II-era destroyer that's been converted into a museum. Visitors can explore the ship's decks, learn about its history, and see a range of artifacts and exhibits related to the war.

For a taste of Louisiana's natural beauty, consider visiting the Bluebonnet Swamp Nature Center, which is located on the outskirts of the city. This beautiful nature preserve offers hiking trails, guided tours, and opportunities to see local wildlife in their natural habitat.

2.3. Shreveport

If you're looking for a taste of Louisiana's unique culture and history, Shreveport is a great place to start. This charming city is located in the northwestern part of the state, and is known for its historic architecture, lively arts scene, and delicious cuisine.

One of the most iconic landmarks in Shreveport is the Texas Street Bridge, a historic bridge that spans the Red River and offers stunning views of the city and the surrounding countryside. Visitors can stroll across the bridge, take in the beautiful scenery, and snap photos of the city's skyline.

Another must-visit attraction in Shreveport is the R.W. Norton Art Gallery, which is home to a stunning collection of European and American art. The museum's collection includes works by some of the most famous artists of the 19th and 20th centuries, including Monet, Renoir, and Degas.

If you're interested in learning about the history of Shreveport, be sure to visit the Shreveport Municipal Auditorium, which played a key role in the development of Louisiana's music scene. The auditorium was the site of Elvis Presley's first live radio broadcast, as well as performances by famous musicians like Johnny Cash and Hank Williams Sr.

For a taste of Louisiana's delicious food culture, consider visiting the Shreveport Farmers' Market, which is held every Saturday and features a wide range of fresh produce, meats, cheeses, and other local specialties. You can also sample some of the city's famous Cajun and Creole dishes at local restaurants like Herby-K's and Marilynn's Place.

2.4. Lafayette

Lafayette is a charming city located in the southwestern part of Louisiana, and is known for its rich history, vibrant arts scene, and delicious cuisine. The city is home to a diverse population of people, including those of Cajun and Creole descent, and this unique culture is reflected in everything from the food to the music.

One of the most popular attractions in Lafayette is the Acadian Cultural Center, which is part of the Jean Lafitte National Historical Park and Preserve. This center offers visitors a chance to learn about the history and culture of the Acadian people, who were forced to leave their homes in Canada and settle in Louisiana in the 18th century. Visitors can explore exhibits, watch films, and attend live music performances that showcase the unique Cajun and Creole traditions of the region.

Another must-visit attraction in Lafayette is the Cathedral of St. John the Evangelist, which is located in the heart of downtown. This beautiful church dates back to the 19th century and features stunning stained-glass windows, intricate woodwork, and other architectural details that are sure to impress.

If you're interested in learning about the local cuisine, Lafayette is a great place to be. The city is known for its delicious Cajun and Creole dishes, including gumbo, jambalaya, and crawfish étouffée. Visitors can sample these dishes at local restaurants like Prejean's and Randol's, or attend one of the many food festivals that take place throughout the year.

For a taste of the local music scene, be sure to check out one of Lafayette's many live music venues. The city is home to a range of talented musicians who specialize in everything from Cajun and zydeco to jazz and blues. Some popular venues include the Blue Moon Saloon and the Heymann Performing Arts Center.

2.5. Lake Charles

Lake Charles is a charming city located in the southwestern part of Louisiana. It is known for its beautiful natural scenery, vibrant arts scene, and delicious food. If you're looking for a relaxing and enjoyable trip, Lake Charles is a great place to be.

One of the most popular attractions in Lake Charles is the Creole Nature Trail, which is a scenic drive that takes you through the beautiful wetlands and wildlife refuges of the area. Along the way, you'll have the chance to see alligators, birds, and other local wildlife, as well as enjoy the stunning natural scenery.

Another must-visit attraction in Lake Charles is the Mardi Gras Museum, which is located in the city's historic district. This museum is dedicated to the history and culture of Mardi Gras, and features colorful costumes, floats, and other artifacts related to this famous Louisiana tradition.

If you're interested in learning about the history of Lake Charles, be sure to visit the Imperial Calcasieu Museum, which is located in the city's downtown area. This museum features exhibits and artifacts related to the history of the region, including its Native American heritage, the oil industry, and the local arts scene.

For a taste of Louisiana's delicious food culture, be sure to visit one of Lake Charles' many excellent restaurants. The city is known for its fresh seafood, delicious steaks, and classic Southern favorites like gumbo and jambalaya. Some popular restaurants include Steamboat Bill's, Luna Bar and Grill, and Darrell's.

3. Top Attractions

In this section, we'll take you through some of the most exciting and unique attractions that Louisiana has to offer, from the historic French Quarter and the colorful Mardi Gras celebration to the natural beauty of the bayous and wetlands.

3.1. French Quarter

The French Quarter is undoubtedly the most famous attraction in Louisiana, and for good reason. This historic neighborhood is home to some of the most iconic landmarks in the state, including Jackson Square, St. Louis Cathedral, and the historic French Market.

One of the best ways to explore the French Quarter is on foot. Take a stroll down the colorful streets and alleyways, and soak up the vibrant energy and unique culture of this iconic neighborhood. You'll find a wide range of shops, restaurants, and cafes to explore, as well as local musicians and street performers who bring the area to life with their music and art.

If you're interested in learning about the history of the French Quarter, be sure to visit some of the neighborhood's many museums and historic sites. The Historic New Orleans Collection is a great place to start, with exhibits and artifacts related to the city's unique history and culture. You can also visit the Cabildo, a historic building that was once the seat of government in colonial Louisiana.

For a taste of the local cuisine, be sure to explore some of the French Quarter's many restaurants and cafes. From classic Creole dishes like gumbo and jambalaya to fresh seafood and po' boy sandwiches, there's something for everyone to enjoy. You can also sample the city's famous beignets and café au lait at Café du Monde, a local institution that's been serving up delicious treats for over 150 years.

Finally, no visit to the French Quarter would be complete without experiencing the nightlife. Bourbon Street is the most famous destination for party-goers, with its lively bars, nightclubs, and music venues. But there are plenty of other places to explore as well, from cozy jazz clubs to elegant cocktail lounges.

3.2. Mardi Gras

If you're planning a trip to Louisiana, you can't miss Mardi Gras. This colorful and exciting event is one of the most famous festivals in the world, and is a true celebration of Louisiana's unique culture and traditions.

Mardi Gras, which means "Fat Tuesday" in French, is a festival that takes place in the weeks leading up to Lent. The festival is known for its elaborate parades, colorful costumes, and lively parties, and is a time for people to let loose and have fun before the more solemn days of Lent.

The heart of Mardi Gras is the city of New Orleans, where the festival has been celebrated for over 300 years. The city's famous parades are organized by "krewes," which are social clubs that plan and fund the parade floats, costumes, and throws.

One of the most iconic features of Mardi Gras is the parade "throws," which are small gifts and trinkets that are tossed from the parade floats to the crowds below. These throws can include everything from beads and doubloons to stuffed animals and decorated coconuts.

In addition to the parades, Mardi Gras is also known for its lively parties and street festivals. The French Quarter is the epicenter of the festivities, with bars and restaurants staying open late into the night and live music filling the streets.

If you're planning to attend Mardi Gras, it's important to plan ahead. The festival is incredibly popular and draws huge crowds, so you'll want to make sure you have accommodations and transportation booked well in advance. You'll also want to make sure you have plenty of cash on hand for food, drinks, and souvenirs.

Finally, it's important to remember that Mardi Gras is a time of celebration, but it's also a time to be respectful and mindful of the local culture and traditions. Be sure to follow the rules and regulations of the parade organizers, and be respectful of the people around you.

3.3. National WWII Museum

If you're interested in learning about the history of World War II, the National WWII Museum in New Orleans is a must-visit destination. This museum is dedicated to telling the story of the war from the American perspective, and features a range of exhibits, artifacts, and interactive displays that bring the history of the war to life.

The museum is divided into several sections, each dedicated to a different aspect of the war. Visitors can explore exhibits related to the war in Europe, the war in the Pacific, and the home front in the United States. There are also exhibits related to D-Day, the Holocaust, and the atomic bomb.

One of the most popular exhibits at the museum is the immersive 4D movie experience "Beyond All Boundaries," which tells the story of the war through the eyes of American soldiers. The movie features stunning visual effects, animatronics, and an all-star cast of narrators, including Tom Hanks and Brad Pitt.

In addition to the exhibits, the museum also offers a range of educational programs and events, including lectures, workshops, and tours. Visitors can also attend special events like the museum's annual Victory Ball, which is held to commemorate the end of World War II.

3.4. Oak Alley Plantation

If you're interested in learning about Louisiana's history, culture, and architecture, be sure to visit the Oak Alley Plantation. This beautiful historic site is located in Vacherie, Louisiana, and is known for its stunning antebellum mansion, beautiful gardens, and rich history.

The Oak Alley Plantation was built in the 1830s and was once a working sugarcane plantation. Today, visitors can explore the grounds, take a guided tour of the mansion, and learn about the history of the people who lived and worked on the plantation.

One of the most iconic features of the Oak Alley Plantation is its stunning entrance, which is lined with a double row of 28 oak trees. These trees are over 300 years old and create a beautiful canopy over the driveway, making for a truly breathtaking sight.

Inside the mansion, visitors can explore the beautiful rooms and learn about the history of the plantation and the people who lived there. The mansion is furnished with period pieces and antiques, giving visitors a glimpse into what life was like in Louisiana in the 19th century.

In addition to the mansion, visitors can also explore the beautiful gardens and grounds of the Oak Alley Plantation. The gardens are home to a wide range of plants and flowers, including camellias, azaleas, and magnolias. There are also several walking trails and picnic areas for visitors to enjoy.

3.5. Bourbon Street

Bourbon Street is one of the most famous attractions in Louisiana, and for good reason. This lively thoroughfare is located in the heart of the French Quarter, and is known for its colorful bars, nightclubs, and live music venues.

If you're looking for a lively and exciting night out in Louisiana, Bourbon Street is the place to be. The street is lined with a wide range of bars and nightclubs, each offering a unique atmosphere and experience. From loud and raucous dance clubs to cozy and intimate jazz bars, there's something for everyone to enjoy on Bourbon Street.

One of the most popular activities on Bourbon Street is bar hopping. Visitors can explore the street's many bars and clubs, sampling a wide range of drinks and enjoying the lively energy of the crowds. Many bars also offer live music performances, ranging from jazz and blues to rock and pop.

In addition to the bars and nightclubs, Bourbon Street is also home to several popular restaurants and cafes. Visitors can sample classic Louisiana dishes like gumbo and jambalaya, as well as fresh seafood and other local specialties.

If you're planning to visit Bourbon Street, it's important to keep a few things in mind. The street can get very crowded, especially on weekends and during peak tourist season. It's also important to be mindful of your surroundings and belongings, as pickpocketing and other crimes can occur in crowded areas.

3.6. Louisiana State Museum

The Louisiana State Museum is an essential destination for anyone interested in the history and culture of Louisiana. The museum is located in the French Quarter of New Orleans, and is dedicated to preserving and showcasing the unique heritage of the state.

The museum features a wide range of exhibits and artifacts that tell the story of Louisiana's past, from its Native American heritage to its role in the Civil War and beyond. Visitors can explore exhibits related to Louisiana's music, art, and literature, as well as its diverse cultural traditions.

One of the most popular exhibits at the Louisiana State Museum is the New Orleans Jazz exhibit, which is dedicated to showcasing the history and evolution of jazz in Louisiana. The exhibit features instruments, recordings, and other artifacts related to the state's vibrant jazz scene, and is a must-visit destination for music lovers.

Another popular exhibit at the museum is the Cabildo, which is a historic building that was once the seat of government in colonial Louisiana. Visitors can explore the building's beautiful architecture and learn about its role in shaping the state's history.

For a taste of Louisiana's unique culture and traditions, be sure to explore the museum's exhibits related to Mardi Gras, Cajun and Creole cuisine, and the state's diverse population of people.

3.7. Preservation Hall

If you're a music lover, no visit to Louisiana would be complete without a trip to Preservation Hall. This legendary music venue is located in the heart of the French Quarter in New Orleans, and is dedicated to preserving and showcasing the city's unique jazz heritage.

Preservation Hall was founded in the 1960s as a way to keep traditional jazz alive in New Orleans. Since then, the venue has become a must-visit destination for anyone who loves jazz, with live performances every night of the week.

The hall itself is an intimate and cozy space, with no air conditioning, no drinks, and no food. The focus here is purely on the music, with some of the most talented jazz musicians in the city taking the stage to perform classic tunes and improvisations.

If you're planning to visit Preservation Hall, it's important to plan ahead. The venue is incredibly popular and can sell out quickly, especially during peak tourist season. You'll want to buy your tickets in advance and arrive early to ensure you get a good seat.

But the effort is well worth it, as a night at Preservation Hall is truly an unforgettable experience. You'll be transported back in time to the golden age of jazz, with the sounds of trumpets, saxophones, and clarinets filling the air and creating a magical atmosphere.

3.8. Tabasco Factory

If you're a fan of spicy food, a visit to the Tabasco Factory on Avery Island is a must-visit destination. This factory is the home of Tabasco sauce, one of the most famous hot sauces in the world, and offers visitors a chance to see how this iconic sauce is made.

The Tabasco Factory tour takes you through the entire process of making Tabasco sauce, from the growing and harvesting of the peppers to the bottling and packaging of the finished product. You'll get a behind-the-scenes look at the factory's production facilities, as well as the chance to sample some of the company's other spicy products.

One of the highlights of the tour is the Tabasco Museum, which is located on the factory grounds. The museum features exhibits and artifacts related to the history of Tabasco sauce, including vintage bottles, advertisements, and packaging.

After the tour, be sure to stop by the Tabasco Country Store, which is located on the factory grounds. Here, you can stock up on all kinds of Tabasco products, including sauces, marinades, and other spicy treats. You can also sample some of the company's other products, including spicy jellies and jams.

3.9. St. Louis Cathedral

St. Louis Cathedral is one of the most iconic landmarks in New Orleans and is a must-visit destination for anyone interested in history, architecture, or religion. This beautiful cathedral is located in the heart of the French Quarter and is a stunning example of Spanish Colonial architecture.

The cathedral dates back to the late 18th century and is named after King Louis IX of France. It has been rebuilt and renovated several times over the years, but still retains much of its original beauty and charm.

Visitors to St. Louis Cathedral can explore the beautiful interior, which features stunning stained-glass windows, intricate woodwork, and other unique architectural details. There are also several chapels and side altars to explore, each with its own unique history and significance.

If you're interested in learning about the history of the cathedral, be sure to take a guided tour. These tours are led by knowledgeable guides who can answer your questions and provide a deeper understanding of the cathedral's significance.

One of the most popular features of St. Louis Cathedral is its beautiful and serene courtyard, which is a peaceful oasis in the heart of the bustling French Quarter. Visitors can take a stroll through the courtyard, admire the beautiful architecture, and enjoy the peaceful atmosphere.

Finally, if you're interested in attending mass, St. Louis Cathedral offers several services throughout the week, including Sunday mass, weekday mass, and special services during holidays and other important occasions.

3.10. Swamp Tours

Louisiana is a state full of culture, history, and natural beauty. Whether you're a foodie looking to sample some of the best seafood and Cajun cuisine in the world, a history buff interested in learning about Louisiana's rich past, or an outdoor enthusiast looking to explore the state's stunning natural scenery, Louisiana has something for everyone.

If you're planning a trip to Louisiana, there are a few things you should keep in mind to make the most of your visit. First and foremost, it's important to be respectful of the local culture and traditions. Louisiana is a state with a unique identity and history, and it's important to be mindful of this as you explore the state.

One of the best ways to experience Louisiana's culture and history is by visiting some of the state's many museums and historic sites. From the National WWII Museum in New Orleans to the Oak Alley Plantation in Vacherie, there are plenty of destinations that will transport you back in time and give you a deeper understanding of Louisiana's past.

Of course, no trip to Louisiana would be complete without sampling some of the state's delicious food. Whether you're in the mood for fresh seafood, spicy gumbo, or a classic po' boy sandwich, there are plenty of restaurants and cafes throughout the state that offer up some of the best cuisine in the world.

But perhaps one of the most unique and exciting aspects of Louisiana is its natural beauty. From the bayous and wetlands of the southern part of the state to the rolling hills and forests of the north, Louisiana is a state full of stunning natural scenery just waiting to be explored. Consider taking a swamp tour to see alligators, birds, and other local wildlife up close, or explore one of the state's many nature preserves or wildlife refuges.

4. Accommodations

Finding the perfect place to stay is an important part of any trip, and Louisiana has a wide range of options to choose from. In this chapter, we'll take you through some of the best accommodation options in Louisiana, from the top hotels and resorts to the best bed and breakfasts and vacation rentals.

4.1. Hotels and Resorts

Louisiana is home to some of the most luxurious hotels and resorts in the world, offering world-class amenities and stunning views of the state's natural beauty. One of the most popular destinations is the Ritz-Carlton New Orleans, located in the heart of the French Quarter. This luxurious hotel features beautiful rooms and suites, a rooftop pool, and a range of dining options, including the famous Domenica restaurant.

Another popular option is the Windsor Court Hotel, which is located just steps from the French Quarter and offers stunning views of the Mississippi River. This elegant hotel features beautifully appointed rooms and suites, a rooftop pool and lounge, and a range of dining options, including the award-winning Grill Room.

For those looking for a more secluded and luxurious experience, the Audubon Cottages are a must-visit destination. Located in the heart of the French Quarter, these beautiful cottages offer a private and intimate escape from the hustle and bustle of the city. Each cottage features a private courtyard, a full kitchen, and beautiful furnishings and decor.

4.2. Bed and Breakfasts

Louisiana is also home to a wide range of cozy and charming bed and breakfasts, offering a more intimate and personal experience for travelers. One of the most popular destinations is the Maison Perrier Bed and Breakfast, located in the beautiful Garden District of New Orleans. This charming inn features beautifully appointed rooms and suites, a beautiful garden, and a range of amenities, including a complimentary breakfast.

Another popular option is the Avenue Inn Bed and Breakfast, also located in the Garden District. This historic inn features beautifully appointed rooms and suites, a beautiful garden, and a range of amenities, including a complimentary breakfast and afternoon tea.

For those looking for a more secluded and romantic experience, the Maison D'Memoire Bed and Breakfast Cottages are a must-visit destination. Located in the beautiful countryside of Lafayette, these beautiful cottages offer a private and intimate escape, with beautiful furnishings and decor, a private hot tub, and a range of amenities, including a complimentary breakfast.

4.3. Vacation Rentals

Louisiana is also home to a wide range of vacation rentals, offering a more flexible and affordable option for travelers. Whether you're looking for a cozy apartment in the heart of New Orleans or a spacious beach house on the Gulf Coast, Louisiana has something to offer every type of traveler.

One of the most popular vacation rental destinations is the French Quarter, where you can find a wide range of apartments and condos available for rent. These properties offer a convenient and affordable option for travelers who want to explore the city on their own terms, with easy access to the city's many attractions and amenities.

Another popular vacation rental destination is the Gulf Coast, where you can find a wide range of beach houses and condos available for rent. These properties offer a secluded and relaxing escape, with stunning views of the Gulf of Mexico and easy access to the region's many beaches and outdoor activities.

4.4. Campgrounds and RV Parks

For those looking for a more rustic and adventurous experience, Louisiana is home to a wide range of campgrounds and RV parks. Whether you're looking for a secluded spot in the woods or a family-friendly campground with plenty of amenities, Louisiana has something to offer every type of camper.

One of the most popular camping destinations is the Kisatchie National Forest, which offers a wide range of camping options, from primitive sites to RV parks with full hookups. This beautiful forest is home to stunning natural beauty and a range of outdoor activities, including hiking, fishing, and wildlife viewing.

Another popular camping destination is the Fontainebleau State Park, located on the shores of Lake Pontchartrain. This beautiful park offers a range of camping options, including tent sites, RV sites, and cabins, as well as a range of amenities, including a swimming pool, a beach, and a nature trail.

5. Food and Drink

In this chapter, we'll take you on a culinary tour of Louisiana, from its famous Cajun and Creole cuisine to its fresh seafood and iconic drinks.

5.1. Traditional Dishes

If you're looking to experience the true flavors of Louisiana, you'll want to start with some of the region's most iconic dishes. Here are just a few of the traditional dishes you won't want to miss:

- **Gumbo:** This hearty soup is a Louisiana classic, made with a roux base, vegetables, and meat or seafood.

- **Jambalaya:** This spicy rice dish is made with a variety of meats and/or seafood, vegetables, and seasonings.
- **Red Beans and Rice:** A staple of Louisiana cuisine, this simple dish is made with red beans, rice, and a variety of meats and seasonings.
- **Crawfish Boil:** A Louisiana tradition, this dish features crawfish, potatoes, corn, and other ingredients boiled together with spices and seasonings.
- **Po' Boys:** These sandwiches are a New Orleans classic, made with French bread and a variety of fillings, from shrimp and oysters to roast beef and gravy.

5.2. Recommended Restaurants

Louisiana is home to a wide range of restaurants, from casual cafes to Michelin-starred fine dining establishments. Here are just a few of the top recommended restaurants in the state:

- **Commander's Palace (New Orleans):** This iconic New Orleans restaurant is known for its elegant atmosphere and award-winning Creole cuisine.

- **Galatoire's (New Orleans):** Another iconic New Orleans establishment, Galatoire's is known for its classic Creole dishes and lively atmosphere.
- **Cochon (New Orleans):** This trendy New Orleans restaurant serves up modern takes on classic Cajun and Creole dishes, with an emphasis on fresh, locally-sourced ingredients.
- **Prejean's (Lafayette):** This classic Cajun restaurant is a must-visit destination for anyone interested in trying traditional Louisiana cuisine.
- **Parrain's Seafood (Baton Rouge):** This Baton Rouge seafood restaurant is known for its fresh seafood and casual atmosphere.

5.3. Recommended Cafes

Louisiana is also home to a wide range of cafes and coffee shops, offering up everything from classic beignets and cafe au lait to modern specialty drinks. Here are just a few of the top recommended cafes in the state:

- **Cafe du Monde (New Orleans):** This iconic New Orleans cafe is known for its classic beignets and cafe au lait, served hot and fresh 24 hours a day.
- **French Truck Coffee (New Orleans):** This trendy New Orleans coffee shop serves up a

variety of specialty coffee drinks, as well as fresh pastries and light bites.

- **Rêve Coffee Roasters (Lafayette):** This Lafayette coffee shop is known for its locally-sourced coffee beans and modern, Instagram-worthy decor.
- **Magpie Cafe (Baton Rouge):** This Baton Rouge cafe is known for its fresh-baked pastries, artisanal coffee drinks, and cozy atmosphere.

6. Shopping

From local markets and shops to high street brands and department stores, there's something for every type of shopper in Louisiana.

6.1. Local Markets and Shops

Louisiana is known for its unique and vibrant local culture, and there's no better way to experience this than by visiting the state's many local markets and shops. Whether you're looking for fresh produce, unique handmade crafts, or one-of-a-kind souvenirs, Louisiana has something to offer every type of shopper.

One of the most iconic markets in Louisiana is the French Market in New Orleans. This historic market dates back to 1791 and is one of the oldest public markets in the country. Here, you can find a wide range of food stalls, souvenir shops, and other vendors selling everything from fresh seafood and produce to handmade crafts and art.

Another popular market in Louisiana is the Lafayette Farmers and Artisans Market at the Horse Farm. This market is held every Saturday morning and features a wide range of local vendors selling fresh produce, handmade crafts, and other unique items. There are also food trucks and live music performances, making it a great place to spend a lazy Saturday morning.

For those looking for a more upscale shopping experience, the Shops at Canal Place in New Orleans are a must-visit destination. This luxury shopping center features a range of high-end retailers, including Saks Fifth Avenue, Michael Kors, and Tory Burch. There are also several gourmet restaurants and cafes, making it a great place to spend an afternoon or evening.

If you're looking for unique and handmade items, there are several artisan markets throughout the state that are worth checking out. One of the most popular is the Arts Market of New Orleans, which is held on the last Saturday of every month in Palmer Park. This market features a wide range of local artists and craftsmen selling everything from jewelry and pottery to paintings and sculptures.

Another great destination for handmade crafts is the Louisiana Crafts Guild, which has several locations throughout the state. This organization promotes the work of local artists and craftsmen, and features a range of unique and beautiful items, including jewelry, ceramics, and textiles.

Of course, no visit to Louisiana would be complete without picking up some of the state's famous hot sauce. There are several hot sauce shops throughout the state, including the Tabasco Company Store on Avery Island and the Louisiana Hot Sauce Shop in New Orleans. These shops offer a range of hot sauces and spicy treats, including rubs, marinades, and other condiments.

6.2. High Street Brands and Department Stores

For those looking for more mainstream shopping options, Louisiana has plenty of high street brands and department stores to choose from. Many of these can be found in shopping centers and malls throughout the state, offering a convenient and comfortable shopping experience.

One of the most popular shopping destinations in Louisiana is the Lakeside Shopping Center in Metairie. This large indoor mall features a range of high street brands and department stores, including Macy's, J.C. Penney, and Dillard's. There are also several restaurants and cafes, as well as a movie theater, making it a great place to spend a day shopping and relaxing.

Another popular shopping destination is the Mall of Louisiana in Baton Rouge. This large shopping center features a range of high street brands and department stores, including H&M, Forever 21, and The Gap. There are also several restaurants and cafes, as well as a movie theater and an indoor amusement park.

If you're looking for a more upscale shopping experience, the Shops at Canal Place in New Orleans are a must-visit destination. This luxury shopping center features a range of high-end retailers, including Saks Fifth Avenue, Michael Kors, and Tory Burch. There are also several gourmet restaurants and cafes, making it a great place to spend an afternoon or evening.

Other popular shopping centers and malls throughout the state include the Acadiana Mall in Lafayette, the Pierre Bossier Mall in Bossier City, and the Tanger Outlets in Gonzales. These shopping centers offer a wide range of high street brands and department stores, as well as a range of dining and entertainment options.

7. Events and Festivals

In this chapter, we'll take you on a tour of some of the state's most iconic events and festivals, from Jazz Fest in New Orleans to the Bayou Country Superfest in Baton Rouge.

7.1. Jazz Fest

Jazz Fest is one of the most iconic events in New Orleans and is a must-visit destination for anyone interested in music, culture, and fun. This annual festival takes place over two weekends in late April and early May and features some of the best music acts from around the world.

The festival takes place in the city's beautiful Fair Grounds Race Course, which is transformed into a sprawling festival ground for the occasion. Visitors can explore multiple stages and areas, each featuring a different musical genre and atmosphere.

The music at Jazz Fest is incredibly diverse, with everything from jazz and blues to rock, pop, and world music on offer. Some of the biggest names in music have performed at the festival over the years, including legends like Aretha Franklin, Ray Charles, and Stevie Wonder.

But Jazz Fest is more than just a music festival. It's also a celebration of Louisiana's unique culture and heritage, with plenty of local food and crafts on offer throughout the festival grounds. Visitors can sample classic Louisiana dishes like gumbo and jambalaya, as well as fresh seafood and other local specialties. There are also plenty of local crafts and souvenirs available for purchase, making it a great place to pick up a unique memento of your trip.

7.2. Essence Festival

The Essence Festival is one of the most iconic and popular events in Louisiana. This annual festival is dedicated to celebrating African American culture and heritage, with a focus on music, art, and community.

The festival takes place over several days in July and features a wide range of events and activities. There are multiple stages featuring live music from some of the biggest names in R&B, hip-hop, and gospel music, as well as workshops and seminars on a variety of topics related to African American culture and community.

One of the highlights of the festival is the Essence Marketplace, which features dozens of vendors selling everything from handmade crafts and jewelry to clothing and accessories. There are also plenty of food vendors offering up classic Louisiana dishes and other tasty treats.

In addition to the music and vendors, the Essence Festival also features a range of community events and activities, including a health and wellness expo, a beauty and style expo, and a family day event featuring games, activities, and entertainment for kids and families.

7.3. Festival International de Louisiane

If you're looking for a truly unique and unforgettable cultural experience, you won't want to miss the Festival International de Louisiane. This annual festival takes place in Lafayette, Louisiana, and is dedicated to celebrating the state's rich French, African, and Caribbean heritage.

The festival takes place over several days in April and features a wide range of events and activities, including live music, dance performances, art exhibits, and food vendors. The music at the festival is incredibly diverse, with everything from Cajun and zydeco to African and Caribbean rhythms on offer.

One of the highlights of the festival is the Parade of Nations, which takes place on the first day of the festival and features colorful floats, costumes, and dancers from around the world. There are also several stages and areas throughout the festival grounds, each featuring a different type of music or performance.

But perhaps the most unique aspect of the Festival International de Louisiane is its focus on Francophone culture. This includes everything from French language workshops and cultural exhibits to traditional French and Cajun food vendors. Visitors can sample classic Louisiana dishes like gumbo and jambalaya, as well as fresh seafood and other local specialties.

7.4. Bayou Country Superfest

If you're a fan of country music, you won't want to miss the Bayou Country Superfest. This annual festival takes place in Baton Rouge and features some of the biggest names in country music, as well as up-and-coming artists and local favorites.

The festival takes place over several days in May and features multiple stages and areas, each featuring a different type of music or atmosphere. Visitors can explore the festival grounds, check out the vendors and food stands, and enjoy live music throughout the day and into the night.

Some of the biggest names in country music have performed at the Bayou Country Superfest over the years, including Blake Shelton, Miranda Lambert, and Luke Bryan. But the festival also features plenty of up-and-coming artists and local favorites, making it a great place to discover new music and support local talent.

In addition to the music, the Bayou Country Superfest also features plenty of food and drink options, including classic Louisiana dishes like gumbo and jambalaya, as well as local craft beer and cocktails. There are also plenty of vendors selling festival merchandise and other souvenirs, making it a great place to pick up a memento of your trip.

8. Nightlife

Are you looking for some fun after the sun goes down? Louisiana's nightlife scene has something for everyone, whether you're in the mood for a quiet drink at a cozy pub or a night of dancing and partying at a lively club.

8.1. Recommended Pubs and Bars

If you're looking for a cozy and intimate spot to grab a drink, Louisiana has plenty of options to choose from. Here are just a few of the top recommended pubs and bars in the state:

- **The Bulldog (New Orleans):** This cozy pub is a favorite among locals and visitors alike. With dozens of craft beers on tap and a cozy patio, it's the perfect spot to relax and unwind after a long day of sightseeing.

- **The Avenue Pub (New Orleans):** This historic pub features a wide range of craft beers, as well as a cozy atmosphere and live music performances throughout the week.
- **The Chimes (Baton Rouge):** This popular Baton Rouge bar and restaurant features a wide range of craft beers and tasty pub food, as well as a lively atmosphere and regular live music performances.
- **The Barley Oak (Mandeville):** This cozy Mandeville pub features a wide range of craft beers and delicious pub fare, as well as a beautiful waterfront patio with stunning views of Lake Pontchartrain.

8.2. Recommended Clubs

If you're in the mood for dancing and partying, Louisiana has plenty of lively clubs and music venues to choose from. Here are just a few of the top recommended clubs in the state:

- **Republic NOLA (New Orleans):** This popular New Orleans club features a wide range of live music performances, as well as regular DJ sets and dance parties.

- **The Varsity Theatre (Baton Rouge):** This historic Baton Rouge music venue features a range of live music performances, as well as regular dance parties and other events.
- **The Howlin' Wolf (New Orleans):** This iconic New Orleans music venue features a range of live music performances, as well as regular dance parties and other events.
- **The Blue Moon Saloon (Lafayette):** This popular Lafayette music venue features a range of live music performances, as well as regular Cajun and zydeco dance parties.

9. Outdoor Activities

Louisiana is home to a wide range of outdoor activities, from fishing and birdwatching to swamp tours and biking.

9.1. Fishing

Louisiana is a paradise for anglers, with a wide range of fishing opportunities available throughout the state. Whether you're a seasoned pro or a novice looking to try your hand at fishing for the first time, Louisiana has something to offer every type of angler.

One of the most popular fishing destinations in Louisiana is the Gulf of Mexico, which is home to a wide range of fish species, including redfish, speckled trout, and tuna. There are several charter fishing companies throughout the state that offer guided fishing trips to the Gulf, providing everything from gear and tackle to expert guidance and advice.

But the Gulf isn't the only place to fish in Louisiana. The state is also home to a wide range of rivers, lakes, and bayous, each offering its own unique fishing opportunities. Some of the most popular freshwater fishing destinations include the Atchafalaya Basin, Toledo Bend Reservoir, and Lake Pontchartrain.

Before heading out on a fishing trip in Louisiana, it's important to make sure you have all the necessary gear and equipment. This includes a fishing license, which can be purchased online or at many local sporting goods stores. You'll also want to make sure you have the right fishing gear and tackle for the type of fishing you're planning to do, as well as appropriate clothing and footwear for the conditions.

It's also important to be aware of local fishing regulations and restrictions. Different species of fish may have different size limits, bag limits, and seasons, and it's important to follow these rules to help protect the state's fish populations and ensure sustainable fishing practices.

9.2. Birdwatching

Louisiana is a birdwatcher's paradise, with a wide range of species available for viewing throughout the state. Whether you're a seasoned birder or a novice looking to try your hand at birdwatching for the first time, Louisiana has something to offer every type of birding enthusiast.

One of the most popular birdwatching destinations in Louisiana is the Atchafalaya Basin, which is home to a wide range of wetland and swamp species, including egrets, herons, and ibises. There are several guided birdwatching tours available throughout the basin, providing expert guidance and advice on the best spots to view these beautiful birds.

Another popular birdwatching destination is the Louisiana State Arboretum, located in Chicot State Park. This beautiful park is home to a range of bird species, including warblers, woodpeckers, and owls. There are several hiking trails throughout the park, providing easy access to the best birding spots.

For those looking for a more challenging birding experience, the Sabine National Wildlife Refuge is a must-visit destination. This beautiful refuge is home to a wide range of bird species, including waterfowl, wading birds, and songbirds. There are several hiking trails and observation platforms throughout the refuge, providing plenty of opportunities to view these beautiful birds in their natural habitat.

Before heading out on a birdwatching trip in Louisiana, it's important to make sure you have the necessary gear and equipment. This includes a good pair of binoculars, a field guide, and appropriate clothing and footwear for the conditions. It's also important to be aware of local regulations and restrictions, as some bird species may be protected or have specific viewing requirements.

In addition to guided tours and observation areas, there are also several birding festivals and events held throughout Louisiana each year. These events provide a great opportunity to connect with other birding enthusiasts and learn more about the state's unique bird species and habitats.

9.3. Hunting

Louisiana is a popular destination for hunters, with a wide range of game species available for hunting throughout the state. If you're planning a hunting trip to Louisiana, there are a few things you should keep in mind to have a safe and successful experience.

First and foremost, it's important to make sure you have all the necessary licenses and permits before heading out on a hunting trip in Louisiana. These licenses and permits can be purchased online or at many local sporting goods stores, and will vary depending on the type of hunting you're planning to do and the species you're targeting.

It's also important to be aware of local hunting regulations and restrictions. Different species of game may have different hunting seasons, bag limits, and other restrictions, and it's important to follow these rules to help protect the state's wildlife populations and ensure sustainable hunting practices.

Before heading out on a hunting trip, it's important to make sure you have the right gear and equipment for the type of hunting you're planning to do. This may include firearms, ammunition, hunting knives, binoculars, and other essential gear. You'll also want to make sure you have appropriate clothing and footwear for the conditions, as well as any necessary safety gear, such as blaze orange clothing.

When hunting in Louisiana, it's important to always prioritize safety. This means following basic gun safety rules, such as keeping your firearm pointed in a safe direction at all times and never pointing it at anyone. It also means being aware of your surroundings and making sure you have a clear line of sight before taking a shot.

If you're planning a hunting trip to Louisiana, it's also recommended that you bring along a hunting guide or experienced local hunter. This can help ensure that you have a safe and successful hunting experience, and can also provide valuable guidance and advice on the best hunting spots and techniques.

9.4. Swamp Tours

One of the most unique and unforgettable experiences you can have in Louisiana is a swamp tour. These tours take you deep into Louisiana's beautiful wetlands, where you can see a wide range of wildlife and plants, including alligators, egrets, and cypress trees.

There are several swamp tour companies throughout the state, offering a range of tour options, from airboat tours to kayak tours. Many tours are led by experienced guides who can provide expert commentary on the history and ecology of the wetlands, as well as point out interesting wildlife and plant species.

One of the most popular swamp tour destinations in Louisiana is the Honey Island Swamp, located just north of New Orleans. This beautiful swamp is home to a wide range of wildlife, including alligators, black bears, and several species of birds. There are several tour companies that offer guided tours of the Honey Island

Swamp, providing a safe and exciting way to explore this unique ecosystem.

Another popular swamp tour destination is the Atchafalaya Basin, which is the largest wetland and swamp area in the United States. This beautiful area is home to a wide range of wildlife, including alligators, otters, and a variety of bird species. There are several tour companies that offer guided tours of the Atchafalaya Basin, providing a unique and unforgettable way to experience this beautiful area.

Before heading out on a swamp tour in Louisiana, it's important to make sure you have the necessary gear and equipment. This may include appropriate clothing and footwear for the conditions, as well as sunscreen and insect repellent. It's also important to be aware of local regulations and restrictions, as some areas of the wetlands may be protected or have specific viewing requirements.

9.5. Biking

If you're looking for a fun and active way to explore Louisiana's beautiful scenery, biking is a great option. With a range of trails and routes available throughout the state, there's something for every type of cyclist, from beginners to experienced riders.

One of the most popular biking destinations in Louisiana is the Tammany Trace, a 31-mile trail that winds through several charming towns and communities on the Northshore of Lake Pontchartrain. The trail is paved and relatively flat, making it an easy and enjoyable ride for cyclists of all skill levels. Along the way, you'll pass through beautiful natural areas, including wetlands, pine forests, and scenic waterways.

Another popular biking destination is the Lafitte Greenway, a 2.6-mile trail that connects the French Quarter to the City Park in New Orleans. The trail is paved and separated from traffic, making it a safe and enjoyable ride for cyclists. Along the way, you'll pass through several vibrant neighborhoods, including Mid-City and Treme, as well as several parks and green spaces.

For those looking for a more challenging ride, the Mississippi River Trail is a must-visit destination. This 3,000-mile trail runs along the length of the Mississippi River, passing through several states, including Louisiana. Along the way, you'll experience a range of landscapes and scenery, from the rolling hills of the Midwest to the swamps and wetlands of Louisiana.

Before heading out on a biking trip in Louisiana, it's important to make sure you have the necessary gear and equipment. This includes a good quality bike, appropriate clothing and footwear for the conditions, and a helmet for safety. It's also important to be aware of local traffic laws and regulations, and to always prioritize safety when biking on roads or in public areas.

In addition to the biking trails and routes, Louisiana also has several biking events and races throughout the year. These events provide a great opportunity to connect with other cyclists and explore new areas of the state. Whether you're looking for a leisurely ride or a challenging race, Louisiana has something to offer every type of cyclist.

10. Additional Information

In this final chapter, we'll provide you with some additional information to help you make the most of your visit to Louisiana.

10.1. Safety Tips

Louisiana is a beautiful and exciting destination, but it's important to always prioritize safety when traveling. Here are a few tips to help you stay safe during your visit:

- Be aware of your surroundings: Louisiana is generally a safe destination, but it's always important to be aware of your surroundings and stay alert, especially when traveling alone or at night.

- Avoid carrying large amounts of cash or valuables: Petty theft can be a problem in some areas of Louisiana, so it's a good idea to avoid carrying large amounts of cash or valuable items with you when out and about.

- Stay hydrated: Louisiana can get hot and humid, especially during the summer months, so it's important to stay hydrated and take frequent breaks when out and about.

- Use sunscreen and insect repellent: The Louisiana sun can be intense, so it's important to use sunscreen to protect your skin. Mosquitoes and other insects can also be a problem in some areas, so it's a good idea to use insect repellent to avoid bites.

- Be cautious when swimming or boating: Louisiana is home to many beautiful waterways, but it's important to always exercise caution when swimming or boating. Follow local safety regulations and be aware of potential hazards, such as strong currents or underwater obstacles.

10.2. Useful Contacts and Emergency Numbers

If you need assistance during your visit to Louisiana, there are several useful contacts and emergency numbers you should be aware of:

- **Emergency services:** In case of emergency, dial 911 from any phone.
- **Tourist assistance:** For tourist assistance, including information on local attractions and events, contact the Louisiana Office of Tourism at 1-800-677-4082.
- **Police department:** For non-emergency police assistance, contact your local police department or sheriff's office.
- **Medical assistance:** For medical assistance, contact your hotel or accommodation for recommendations on local medical facilities.

10.3. Online Resources

There are several online resources available to help you plan your visit to Louisiana:

- **Louisiana Office of Tourism:** The Louisiana Office of Tourism website is a great resource for information on local attractions, events, and accommodations. Visit them at https://www.louisianatravel.com/.
- **Visit New Orleans:** The Visit New Orleans website is a great resource for information on

local attractions, events, and accommodations in New Orleans. Visit them at https://www.neworleans.com/.

- **Louisiana State Parks:** The Louisiana State Parks website is a great resource for information on local parks and natural areas, including hiking trails, camping facilities, and more. Visit them at https://www.crt.state.la.us/louisiana-state-parks/.

Printed in Great Britain
by Amazon

23369219R00040